MW01517876

A gift for:

_____

I have not stopped giving thanks for you,
remembering you in my prayers.

EPHESIANS 1:16

From:

_____

Prayers for a Woman's Soul Journal
Copyright © 2006 by The Zondervan Corporation
ISBN-10: 0-310-81014-0
ISBN-13: 978-0-310-81014-8

Requests for information should be addressed to:
Inspirio, The gift group of Zondervan
Grand Rapids, Michigan 49530
http://www.inspiriogifts.com

Compiler: Snapdragon Editorial Group, Inc
Project Manager: Tom Dean
Design Manager: Jody Langley
Design: Pamela J. L. Eicher
Production Management: Matt Nolan

Printed in China
06 07 08/4 3 2 1

Prayers
FOR A
Woman's Soul

JOURNAL

inspirio™

How great is the love the Father has lavished on us, that we should be called children of God! And that is what we are!

1 JOHN 3:1

Lord: Grant me the trusting heart of a child that I might come into your presence and simply accept your gift of love already given. *Amen.*

Rosalind Rinker

God is love. Whoever lives in love lives in God, and God in him. In this way, love is made complete among us so that we will have confidence on the day of judgment, because in this world we are like him.

1 JOHN 4:16–17

_____
_____
_____
_____
_____
_____
_____
_____
_____
_____
_____
_____
_____
_____
_____
_____
_____
_____
_____
_____

Lord, Because you love me, I always have love to give away to anyone who crosses my path. *Amen.*

Barbara Johnson

_____

_____

_____

_____

_____

_____

_____

_____

_____

_____

_____

_____

_____

_____

_____

_____

_____

_____

_____

_____

_____

Love is patient, love is kind. It does not envy, it does not boast, it is not proud. It is not rude, it is not self-seeking, it is not easily angered, it keeps no record of wrongs.

1 CORINTHIANS 13:4–5

Lord: Help me to be patient and kind toward others. Help me not to boast when I'm right or be proud when others are wrong. Help me not to be rude. I don't want my love to be self-seeking, or easily angered. And, Lord, convict me if I start keeping a record of wrongs. *Amen.*

Joni Eareckson Tada

His divine power has given us everything we need for life and godliness through our knowledge of him who called us by his own glory and goodness.

_____

_____

_____

_____

_____

_____

_____

_____

_____

_____

_____

_____

_____

_____

_____

_____

_____

_____

_____

_____

_____

Lord: May I contentedly serve you, love you, and luxuriate in what you empower me to do in your name and for your sake. *Amen.*

Marilyn Meberg

Because of his great love for us, God, who is rich in mercy, made us alive with Christ even when we were dead in transgressions—it is by grace you have been saved.

EPHESIANS 2:4–5

_____

_____

_____

_____

_____

_____

_____

_____

_____

_____

_____

_____

_____

_____

_____

_____

_____

_____

_____

_____

_____

Lord: Your marvelous love has set me free from the guilt and consequences of my sin. I rejoice and am humbled by your abundant forgiveness. *Amen.*

Fern Nichols

God demonstrates his love for us in this: While we were still sinners, Christ died for us.

ROMANS 5:8

Lord: What a risk you took loving me. Give me the wisdom and courage to risk loving you in return. *Amen.*

Patsy Clairmont

_____
_____
_____
_____
_____
_____
_____
_____
_____
_____
_____
_____
_____
_____
_____
_____
_____
_____
_____
_____
_____
_____

*No matter how many promises God has made, they are "Yes"
in Christ. And so through him the "Amen" is spoken by us to
the glory of God.*

2 CORINTHIANS 1:20

Lord, Thank you for your precious promises. Thank you for your powerful Word. Thank you for your enabling Holy Spirit. Thank you for your patient love. *Amen.*

Nancy Kennedy

I can do everything through Christ who gives me strength.

PHILIPPIANS 4:13

_____

_____

_____

_____

_____

_____

_____

_____

_____

_____

_____

_____

_____

_____

_____

_____

_____

_____

_____

_____

Lord, I know that if you lead me to do something, you will provide the necessary strength, even the strength to do something I really don't want to do. When I lack the willingness and the conviction, please change my heart. *Amen.*

Nancy Kennedy

How great is your goodness,
*   which you have stored up for those who fear you,*
which you bestow in the sight of men.
*   on those who take refuge in you.*

PSALM 31:19

_____

_____

_____

_____

_____

_____

_____

_____

_____

_____

_____

_____

_____

_____

_____

_____

_____

_____

_____

_____

_____

Lord, I want to rise like the sun, in your strength, and shine for your glory. Because I know your goodness and your mercy, I offer myself to you as an act of worship. *Amen.*

Nancy Kennedy

You, O LORD, keep my lamp burning;
  my God turns my darkness into light.

PSALM 18:28

Lord: Come and enlighten the darkness of my heart. Give me right faith, certain hope, and perfect love that everything I do may be in fulfillment of your holy will; through Jesus Christ my Lord. *Amen.*

Saint Francis of Assisi

I pray also that the eyes of your heart may be enlightened in order that you may know the hope to which he has called you, the riches of his glorious inheritance in the saints.

EPHESIANS 1:18

_____

_____

_____

_____

_____

_____

_____

_____

_____

_____

_____

_____

_____

_____

_____

_____

_____

_____

_____

_____

Lord, Grant me to know what is worth knowing, to love what is worth loving, to praise what delights you most, to value what is precious to you, and to reject whatever is evil in your eyes. *Amen.*

Thomas à Kempis

In his heart a man plans his course,
*but the L*ORD *determines his steps.*

PROVERBS 16:9

_____

_____

_____

_____

_____

_____

_____

_____

_____

_____

_____

_____

_____

_____

_____

_____

_____

_____

_____

_____

_____

_____

Lord: Guide me along your way, and help me to piece together the jigsaw of life in your kingdom. *Amen.*

Author Unknown

Encourage one another and build each other up, just as in fact you are doing.

1 THESSALONIANS 5:11

_____

_____

_____

_____

_____

_____

_____

_____

_____

_____

_____

_____

_____

_____

_____

_____

_____

_____

_____

_____

_____

Lord: Quicken my spirit that I may be able to
encourage the souls of all who journey with me on
the road of life, to your honor and glory. *Amen.*

Saint Augustine of Hippo

Since you are my rock and my fortress,
for the sake of your name lead and guide me.

Psalm 31:3

Lord: Give me faith to go out with a good courage, not knowing where I am going, but only that your hand is leading me, and your love supporting me; to the glory of your name. *Amen.*

Eric Milner—White & G.W. Griggs

Show me your ways, O LORD,
teach me your paths;
guide me in your truth and teach me,
for you are God my Savior,
and my hope is in you all day long.

PSALM 25:4–5

Lord: Grant me in all my doubts and uncertainties the grace to ask what you would have me do; that the Spirit of wisdom may save me from all false choices, and that in your light I may see light; through Jesus Christ my Lord. *Amen.*

William Bright

The path of the righteous is level;
  O upright One, you make the way of the righteous
    smooth.

ISAIAH 26:7

Lord: Be now a bright flame to enlighten me, a guiding star to lead me, a smooth path beneath my feet, and a kindly shepherd along my way, today and for evermore. *Amen.*

Saint Columba

Lord: Forgive me for what I have been, sanctify what I am, and order what I shall be. *Amen.*

Frederick MacNutt

It is God who works in you to will and to act according to his good purpose.

PHILIPPIANS 2:13

Lord: I pray for a spirit that is willing to be used in your kingdom work. Show me where you want me to serve you. Show me how you want me to do your work. *Amen*

Denise George

Create in me a pure heart, O God,
and renew a steadfast spirit within me.

PSALM 51:10

Lord: Give me a steadfast heart, which no unworthy affection may drag downwards; give me an unconquered heart, which no tribulation can wear out; give me an upright heart, which no unworthy purpose may tempt aside. *Amen.*

Saint Thomas Aquinas

Hope does not disappoint us, because God has poured out his love into our hearts by the Holy Spirit, whom he has given us.

ROMANS 5:5

Lord, Help me look at life in a fresh, exciting way, different from before, being assured that you do not disappoint. I praise you for what you will do in my life today, and I can't wait to see it happen. *Amen.*

Luci Swindoll

_____

_____

_____

_____

_____

_____

_____

_____

_____

_____

_____

_____

_____

_____

_____

_____

_____

_____

_____

_____

_____

_____

_____

_____

Dear friend, I pray that you may enjoy good health and that all may go well with you, even as your soul is getting along well.

3 JOHN 2

Lord: Grant me health and peacefulness, fun and friendship, a warm and welcoming spirit, and the gentleness that quickly forgives, now and always. *Amen.*

Author Unknown

_____
_____
_____
_____
_____
_____
_____
_____
_____
_____
_____
_____
_____
_____
_____
_____
_____
_____
_____
_____
_____
_____
_____
_____

Jesus said, "If you love those who love you, what reward will you get? Are not even the tax collectors doing that? And if you greet only your brothers, what are you doing more than others? Do not even pagans do that?"

MATTHEW 5:46–47

Lord: When I want to ignore or move away from people I don't understand, help me to listen to my instincts and not to miss out on some of the best blessings even when they come in unusual packages. *Amen.*

Thelma Wells

Love keeps no record of wrongs. ... It always protects, always trusts, always hopes, always perseveres.

1 CORINTHIANS 13:5, 7

Lord: Give me, I pray you, a mind forgetful of past injury, a will to seek the good of others and a heart of love. *Amen.*

A New Zealand Prayer Book

Teach me your way, O LORD,
and I will walk in your truth;
give me an undivided heart,
that I may fear your name.

PSALM 86:11

Lord, what I know not, teach me.
Lord, what I have not, give me.
Lord, what I am not, make me.
Amen.

Saint Augustine of Hippo

Be completely humble and gentle; be patient, bearing with one another in love.

EPHESIANS 4:2

Lord: Help me to listen to others, be gentle with others, forgive others and be willing to laugh at myself. *Amen.*

Author Unknown

Each of you should look not only to your own interests, but also to the interests of others.

PHILIPPIANS 2:4

_____

_____

_____

_____

_____

_____

_____

_____

_____

_____

_____

_____

_____

_____

_____

_____

_____

_____

_____

_____

_____

_____

Lord. Teach me to forget myself and love others.
Amen.

Sheila Walsh

My dear brothers, take note of this: Everyone should be quick to listen, slow to speak and slow to become angry, for man's anger does not bring about the righteous life that God desires.

JAMES 1:19–20

Lord: You are my champion. Teach me to value people even more than the tantalizing last word. May I lean in and truly hear what others are saying. *Amen.*

Patsy Clairmont

You have made known to me the path of life;
you will fill me with joy in your presence,
with eternal pleasures at your right hand.

PSALM 16:11

Lord, Help me encourage others to lean on you when they seem discouraged by this world's troubles. Let me be an example by seeking comfort and peace in Jesus' presence. For in his presence is joy beyond measure. *Amen.*

Thelma Wells

Jesus said, "What is impossible with men is possible with God."

LUKE 18:27

Lord: Never let me be afraid to pray for the impossible. *Amen.*

Dorothy Shellenberger

Jesus said, "Come to me, all you who are weary and burdened, and I will give you rest. Take my yoke upon you and learn from me, for I am gentle and humble in heart, and you will find rest for your souls."

MATTHEW 11:28–29

Lord, Time is in your hands. Remind me to relax so I can be part of anything amazing you might want to do through me or for me. *Amen.*

Joni Eareckson Tada

I have set the LORD always before me.
    Because he is at my right hand,
I will not be shaken.
    Therefore my heart is glad and my tongue rejoices;
my body also will rest secure.

PSALM 16:8–9

Lord, You are the source of my peace, the foundation upon which my security rests, and the inspiration for finding gladness in the daily routine of my life. May I experience more God-given gladness as I celebrate the days you have ordained for me here on earth. *Amen.*

Marilyn Meberg

Be very careful, then, how you live—not as unwise but as wise, making the most of every opportunity.

_____

_____

_____

_____

_____

_____

_____

_____

_____

_____

_____

_____

_____

_____

_____

_____

_____

_____

_____

_____

Lord, Give me the grace today to take time. Time
to be with you. Time to be with others. Time to
enjoy the life you have given me. Help me remember
that today is the day you have made. May I rejoice
and be glad in it! *Amen.*

Luci Swindoll

Jesus said, "I have come that they may have life, and have it to the full."

JOHN 10:10

Lord: Because of your life in me, each moment of my life has value and potential for significance—if I will only celebrate it. Infuse my attitude with the fruit of your Spirit, patience. *Amen.*

Barbara Johnson

Though you have not seen him, you love him; and even though you do not see him now, you believe in him and are filled with an inexpressible and glorious joy.

1 PETER 1:8

_____

_____

_____

_____

_____

_____

_____

_____

_____

_____

_____

_____

_____

_____

_____

_____

_____

_____

_____

_____

_____

Lord: Grant me a deeper knowledge of the joy which is mine in Christ Jesus, that here my heart may be glad, and in the world to come my joy may be full: for with the Son and the Holy Spirit, you are my God, now and for ever. *Amen.*

Raymond Hockley

Banish anxiety from your heart
  and cast off the troubles of your body.

ECCLESIASTES 11:10

_____

_____

_____

_____

_____

_____

_____

_____

_____

_____

_____

_____

_____

_____

_____

_____

_____

_____

_____

_____

_____

Lord: Teach me to banish anxiety from my heart and cast off the troubles of my body. Create within me a lightness of being that comes from knowing you. *Amen.*

Marilyn Meberg

He will be the sure foundation for your times,
    a rich store of salvation and wisdom and knowledge;
the fear of the LORD is the key to this treasure.

ISAIAH 33:6

_____
_____
_____
_____
_____
_____
_____
_____
_____
_____
_____
_____
_____
_____
_____
_____
_____
_____
_____
_____
_____
_____
_____

Lord, make me aware of your precious treasure that is all around me. Your Word says you have given me more than enough. I celebrate my heritage as your child. *Amen.*

Barbara Johnson

My people will live in peaceful dwelling places,
in secure homes,
in undisturbed places of rest.

ISAIAH 32:18

Lord: You provide my safety, my security, my eternal hope. Because of those loving assurances, enable me to see the joy and feel the joy. Thank you that you are my reason for joy each day. *Amen.*

Marilyn Meberg

All the days of the oppressed are wretched,
but the cheerful heart has a continual feast.

_____
_____
_____
_____
_____
_____
_____
_____
_____
_____
_____
_____
_____
_____
_____
_____
_____
_____
_____
_____
_____
_____

Lord: Help me to be generous with my giggles and sparse with my frowns. *Amen.*

Patsy Clairmont

A cheerful heart is good medicine,
but a crushed spirit dries up the bones.

PROVERBS 17:22

Lord: Help me to rise up out of the dark corners of my soul and believe you have indeed provided medicine for joyful healing. May I take at least one dose every day. *Amen.*

Marilyn Meberg

If you, O LORD, kept a record of sins,
    O Lord, who could stand?
But with you there is forgiveness;
    therefore you are feared.

_____

_____

_____

_____

_____

_____

_____

_____

_____

_____

_____

_____

_____

_____

_____

_____

_____

_____

_____

_____

_____

_____

_____

Lord: When I make mistakes, remind me it isn't the end of the world. It's a learning experience, an opportunity to laugh and to trust your sovereignty. *Amen.*

Luci Swindoll

If, when we were God's enemies, we were reconciled to him through the death of his Son, how much more, having been reconciled, shall we be saved through his life! Not only is this so, but we also rejoice in God through our Lord Jesus Christ, through whom we have now received reconciliation.

ROMANS 5:10–11

Lord: Because of the cross, I have been reconciled to you for now and eternity. Because of that truth I do indeed break forth with rejoicing and shouts of joy. *Amen.*

Marilyn Meberg

I praise you because I am fearfully and wonderfully made;
your works are wonderful,
I know that full well.

PSALM 139:14

Lord: What a wonderful feeling it is that I don't have to be someone else ... and they don't have to be me. You have called us each to be ourselves. Help me find the joy today in being me. *Amen.*

Luci Swindoll

Now that you have been set free from sin and have become slaves to God, the benefit you reap leads to holiness, and the result is eternal life.

ROMANS 6:22

Lord: Because you have given me the gift of salvation through your death on the cross, I have been set free from the weight of sin. I can enter into new experiences with ease and gratitude, and give you praise for these earthly pleasures. *Amen.*

Marilyn Meberg

Jesus said, "You are the light of the world.... In the same way, let your light shine before men, that they may see your good deeds and praise your Father in heaven."

MATTHEW 5:14, 16

Lord: Grant me the trusting heart of a child that I might come into your presence and simply accept the gift of love already given. Fill me with your Holy Spirit that I might become like a shining light of truth in this dark world. *Amen.*

Rosalind Rinker

The LORD *is near to all who call on him,*
to all who call on him in truth.

PSALM 145:18

Lord, I am weak and often fail. But, oh, what glory it is to be able to talk with you, to know you are near, that you care. I love you, Lord, with all my heart. *Amen.*

Rosalind Rinker

We are God's workmanship, created in Christ Jesus to do good works, which God prepared in advance for us to do.

EPHESIANS 2:10

_____

_____

_____

_____

_____

_____

_____

_____

_____

_____

_____

_____

_____

_____

_____

_____

_____

_____

_____

_____

Lord, I am who I am by your loving design. Help me to accept my weaknesses as well as my strengths. Help me, too, to embrace myself in my totality as you embrace me, knowing I cannot do what was not ordained for me. *Amen.*

Marilyn Meberg

Trust in the LORD with all your heart
and lean not on your own understanding;
in all your ways acknowledge him,
and he will make your paths straight.

PROVERBS 3:5–6

Lord, Forgive me for leaning on my own understanding when the road gets rough. I acknowledge today that I am not promised an easy path, just a straight one if I trust entirely in You. With every pothole, rut, or barrier I may come across, help me to remember to lean on You. *Amen.*

Joni Eareckson Tada

See, I am doing a new thing!
        Now it springs up; do you not perceive it?
I am making a way in the desert
        and streams in the wasteland.

ISAIAH 43:19

Lord: Thank you that you can create something beautiful out of what appears to be dead. You do it every day. I'm grateful for your creative ideas that cost nothing but demonstrate your love for me. *Amen.*

Luci Swindoll

The LORD appeared to us in the past, saying:
"I have loved you with an everlasting love;
    I have drawn you with loving-kindness."

JEREMIAH 31:3

Lord: When my love grows thin, yours is abundant for me, in me, and through me. And because your love is forbearing, I can likewise forbear. I can go on ... patiently. You never said it would be easy, but you did say it would be possible. *Amen.*

Author Unknown

This is my prayer: that your love may abound more and more in knowledge and depth of insight, so that you may be able to discern what is best and may be pure and blameless until the day of Christ.

PHILIPPIANS 1:9–10

_____
_____
_____
_____
_____
_____
_____
_____
_____
_____
_____
_____
_____
_____
_____
_____
_____
_____
_____
_____
_____
_____
_____

Lord: Give me true discernment, so that I may judge rightly between things that differ. Above all, may I search out and do what is pleasing to you through Jesus Christ my Lord. *Amen.*

Thomas à Kempis

I trust in your unfailing love;
    my heart rejoices in your salvation.
I will sing to the LORD,
    for he has been good to me.

PSALM 13:5

Lord: Forgive me for not trusting you when I am in crisis. In those moments I find myself feeling frustrated, angry, or scared, I forget you are a good God and everything you allow to happen in my life is for a purpose. Forgive me for allowing my problems to control my thoughts and actions instead of trusting in your goodness for me. *Amen.*

Fern Nichols

Whether you turn to the right or to the left, your ears will hear a voice behind you, saying, "This is the way; walk in it."

ISAIAH 30:21

Lord: When I make decisions, lead me to the heart of the matter, and when I face conflict, do not let my own panic drown out the still, small voice of your wisdom. *Amen.*

Author Unknown

Send forth your light and your truth,
let them guide me;
let them bring me to your holy mountain,
to the place where you dwell.

PSALM 43:3

Lord, You are both the light and the guide of those who put their trust in you. *Amen.*

Author Unknown

I am still confident of this:
    I will see the goodness of the LORD
in the land of the living.

PSALM 27:13

Lord: Grant me a heart wide open to all your joy and beauty, and save my soul from being so steeped in care, or so darkened by passion, that I pass heed-less and unseeing when even the thornbush by the wayside is aflame with the glory of God. *Amen.*

Walter Rauschenbusch

I am always with you;
*   you hold me by my right hand.*
You guide me with your counsel,
*   and afterward you will take me into glory.*

PSALM 73:23–24

Lord: Let me hold your hand and like a child walk with you down all my days, secure in your love and strength. *Amen.*

Thomas à Kempis

The Lord said to me, "My grace is sufficient for you, for my power is made perfect in weakness." Therefore I will boast all the more gladly about my weaknesses, so that Christ's power may rest on me.

2 CORINTHIANS 12:9

Lord: Enable me to bear up under my burden by your grace. Help me to remember that you have handpicked my circumstances to accomplish your purposes for my life. May I humbly submit to your choice for me. *Amen.*

Joni Eareckson Tada

We know also that the Son of God has come and has given us understanding, so that we may know him who is true. And we are in him who is true—even in his Son Jesus Christ. He is the true God and eternal life.

1 JOHN 5:20

Lord, I want to want you: I long to be filled with longing; I thirst to be made more thirsty still. Show me your glory, I pray, that so I may know you indeed. Begin in mercy a new work of love within me. *Amen.*

A. W. *Tozer*

The LORD *says,*
"Before they call I will answer;
 while they are still speaking I will hear."

ISAIAH 65:24

Lord, Thank you for always keeping your communication line open. Your listening ear is my source of comfort. *Amen.*

Thelma Wells

A righteous man may have many troubles,
but the LORD delivers him from them all.

PSALM 34:19

Lord: Set me free in the glory of your will, so that I will only as you will. Your will be at once your perfection and mine. You alone are deliverance and absolute safety from every cause and kind of trouble that ever existed, anywhere now exists, or ever can exist in your universe. *Amen.*

George Macdonald

Pray in the Spirit on all occasions with all kinds of prayers and requests. With this in mind, be alert and always keep on praying for all the saints.

EPHESIANS 6:18

Lord: Protect those whom I love and who are separated from me. Guide them when they are uncertain, comfort them when they are lonely or afraid, and bless them with the warmth of your presence. *Amen.*

Author Unknown

Now that you have purified yourselves by obeying the truth so that you have sincere love for your brothers, love one another deeply, from the heart.

1 PETER 1:22

Lord: As I stuff my bags full of goodies (peace, patience, love, joy), may we then share them lavishly. Thank you for always sticking by me. *Amen.*

Patsy Clairmont

Jesus said, "In everything, do to others what you would have them do to you, for this sums up the Law and the Prophets."

MATTHEW 7:12

Lord: Spirit of truth, help me to be truthful with with others. Lord, who knows what is in my heart more clearly than I do myself, help me to hear others. *Amen.*

Richard Harries

At Inspirio, we love to hear from you—your
stories, your feedback,
and your product ideas.
Please send your comments to us
by way of email at
icares@zondervan.com
or to the address below:

inspirio
Attn: Inspirio Cares
5300 Patterson Avenue SE
Grand Rapids, MI 49530
If you would like further information
about Inspirio and the products we
create please visit us at:
www.inspiriogifts.com
Thank you and God bless!